# *Nita Mehta's*
# Mughlai
# Cooking

## *Nita Mehta*

**B.Sc. (Home Scie      ), M.Sc. (Food and Nutrition), Gold Medalist**

**&**

## TANYA MEHTA

**SNAB**
Publishers Pvt Ltd

*Nita Mehta's*
# Mughlai
### Cooking
© Copyright 2002 **SNAB** Publishers Pvt Ltd

First Edition 2002
ISBN 81-7869-035-7

*Food Styling and Photography:* **SNAB**

*Layout and laser typesetting :*

National Information
Technology Academy
3A/3, Asaf Ali Road
New Delhi-110002
**N.I.T.A.**
☎ 3252948

*Published by :*

**SNAB**
**Publishers Pvt. Ltd.**
3A/3 Asaf Ali Road,
New Delhi - 110002
Tel: 3252948, 3250091
Telefax:91-11-3250091

Editorial and Marketing office:
**E-348, Greater Kailash-II, N.Delhi-48**
*Fax:*91-11-6235218 *Tel:*91-11-6214011, 6238727
*E-Mail:* nitamehta@email.com
snab@snabindia.com
*Website:*http://www.nitamehta.com
*Website:* http://www.snabindia.com

*Distributed by :*

THE VARIETY BOOK DEPOT
A.V.G. Bhavan, M 3 Con Circus,
New Delhi - 110 001
Tel : 3327175,  3322567; Fax : 3714335

*Printed by :*

THOMSON PRESS (INDIA) LIMITED

**Rs. 89/-**

# *Introduction*

$\mathcal{E}$ven today, the North Indian food reflects the influence of the Mughals of the 16th century. Mughlai food is rich, flavourful and fragrant.

Mughlai recipes lay stress on rich ingredients like almonds, cashews, pista etc. The food is usually cooked on low flame with flavourful spices added to it. Whole spices such as cardamoms, cinnamon, cloves, mace and nutmeg are some of the spices that impart a subtle flavour to Mughlai food.

Curd and cream form the gravies having less stress on tomatoes. Onions are usually deep fried to a golden brown colour and then blended to a paste.

The popular dishes that influence Mughlai cooking are the Kormas in creamy sauces and the koftas slowly cooked in rich sauces. Kebabs are the speciality of Mughlai cooking and served as snacks as well as meal time accompaniments. "Biryani", holds a special place in Mughlai food.

*Nita Mehta*

# *Contents*

## Mehfil-e-Kebab & Tandoori   10

# Dil Bahar-e-Murg/Gosht 34
## (Chicken & Mutton Main Dishes)

Murg Nizam    35

Gosht Khada Masala    38

Makhani Murg (Butter Chicken)    40

Haryali chicken    42

Shahi Kaju Murg    44

Shahjehani Gosht    46

Mutton Malai Kofta    49

Achaari Korma    52

Shahi Meat    54

Piste Waala Murg    56

# Gulbahaar-e-Subz 59
## (Vegetables)

Methi Malai Khumb Matar    60

Shahi Baby Corns    62

Safed Mughlai Paneer    66

Dal Makhani    68

Haryali Kofta    70

Gobhi Mussallam    72

Manzil-e-Paneer    76

Baghare Baingan    78

8

# Biryani & Rotis   81

## VEGETARIAN
Subz Masala Pulao   88

Khumb Biryani   90

Missi Roti   93

Lachha Parantha   94

## NON-VEGETARIAN
Mutton Biryani   82

Hyderabadi Murg Biryani   84

Tandoori Keema Parantha   96

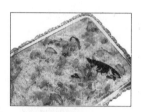

# Meetha   98

Baadami Sewian Kheer   99

Shahi Tukri   100

Kesar Kulfi   102

# Mehfil-e-Kebab
# & Tandoori

# *Boti Din Raat*

*Delicious mutton kebabs served in boiled eggs.*

*Serves 8-10*

250 gms mutton (boneless) - cut into 1" pieces

**1ST MARINADE**
1 tbsp lemon juice
3 tbsp ginger-garlic paste

**2ND MARINADE**
¼ tsp saffron (kesar), ½ tsp milk
1 cup thick curd - tie in a muslin cloth & hang for 1 hour
1 tbsp kachri powder or 1 tbsp raw papaya paste (kachha papita) - peel, deseed
and grind a small piece of raw papaya in a mixer
¼ tsp soda-bicarbonate (mitha soda)
2 onions - cut into slices, deep fried till golden and ground to a paste
½ tsp green cardamom powder (chhoti illaichi), 1 tsp salt, 1 tsp pepper powder

*contd...*

## TO SERVE
5 hard boiled eggs - halved and egg yolk separated from egg white

1. Soak the kesar in ½ tsp milk for a few minutes.
2. Cut the mutton into 1" cubes. Wash and pat dry the pieces. Prick them with a fork. Mix lemon juice and ginger-garlic paste with the mutton cubes. Keep aside for half an hour.
3. Mix all the ingredients of 2nd marinade- kesar, curd, papaya paste or kachri powder, mitha soda, fried onion paste, chhoti illaichi, salt and pepper.
4. Add marinated mutton to the second marinade mixture. Mix thoroughly. Let the mutton marinate in this for atleast 4 hours or even more in the refrigerator.
5. To cook the botis, remove from fridge and let them come to room temperature. Heat an electric oven at 150°C or a gas tandoor on gas at moderate flame. Thread 5 to 6 pieces of mutton onto each greased skewer or place the botis on a greased wire rack of the oven. Rub with the left over marinade

6. Grill for 15- 20 minutes turning them 2 to 3 times inbetween. When slightly dry, spoon or brush some (about 2 tbsp) oil on them. Cook for another 10 minutes or till done. Remove the tikkas from the skewer.
7. Hard boil the eggs. Cool, peel and cut into half widthwise. Remove the egg yolk from the egg white. Put a piece of tikka in the hollowed egg.
8. Sprinkle garam masala. Serve hot with dahi-poodina chutney and onion rings seasoned with salt, red chilli powder and lime juice.

**Note:**
- An interesting side dish from the boiled egg yolks to be served along: Chop the 5 boiled egg yolks coarsely and mix lightly with 1 finely chopped onion, 2 chopped green chillies, 1 tbsp chopped coriander and 1 tsp oil. Sprinkle some salt and pepper. Add 1 tbsp lemon juice. Mix well and serve.
- Grilling or roasting should be done on constant moderate heat, otherwise it toughens the protein of the meat, making the kebabs shrink and turn hard.

# *Hare Chholia ke Kebab*

*There are unlimited combinations for making vegetable kebabs. Here hara chholia has been used to churn out deliciously succulent kebabs.*

### Makes 14

2 cups fresh green gram (hare chholia)
½ cup besan (gramflour) - roasted on a tawa for 1 minute, or till fragrant
2 slices bread - broken into pieces and churned in a mixer to get fresh crumbs
1 cup yogurt - hang in a muslin cloth for 30 minutes
1 small onion - chopped, 1 tbsp ginger-garlic paste
3-4 green chillies - chopped
10-12 fresh curry leaves, 1 tbsp tandoori masala
1 tsp salt  or to taste, 1 tsp jeera
3 tbsp oil plus oil for shallow frying
2-3 tbsp maida (plain flour)

**CRUSH TOGETHER**
1 tbsp saboot dhania (coriander seeds), 1 tsp roasted jeera (bhuna jeera)
½ tsp saboot kali mirch (black peppercorns)

1. Crush saboot dhania, bhuna jeera and saboot kali mirch on a chakla-belan (rolling board-pin).
2. Clean, wash hare chholia. Pressure cook hare chholia with the above crushed spices, ½ tsp salt and 1 cup water. Give one whistle. Remove from fire and keep aside. After the pressure drops down, mash the hot hare chholia with a potato masher or a karchhi. If there is any water, mash and dry the chholia on fire. Remove from fire.
3. Heat 3 tbsp oil, add jeera, let it change colour. Add chopped onion, ginger-garlic paste, chopped green chillies and curry leaves. Cook till onions turn light brown.
4. Add mashed chholia, pepper, salt, roasted besan, tandoori masala & hung yogurt. Cook for 5 minutes or till dry. Remove from fire. Cool.
5. Add bread crumbs and mix well.
6. Make marble sized balls of the chholia mixture. Flatten to form a kebab of about 2" diameter.
7. Roll in maida and shallow fry 3-4 pieces at a time on a hot tawa in 6 tbsp oil. Turn sides and fry till both sides are crisp. Remove the kebabs on paper napkins. Serve.

# Mewa Seekh

*Delicious rich seekh kebabs for special occasions.*

*Picture on cover*                    *Serves 4 - 5*

½ kg (500 gm) keema (chicken mince)
1 cup dry bread crumbs, 1 tsp oil, 1 tbsp cornflour, ½ tsp garam masala
½ tsp salt, 1 tsp magaz (melon seeds), 1 tbsp chironji (sunflower seeds)

### GRIND TOGETHER

1" piece ginger, 6-8 flakes garlic, 2 green chillies, ¼ cup green coriander
1½ tbsp kaju (cashewnuts), 6 badam (almonds) - blanched and peeled
5 kishmish (raisins), ½ tsp whole pista (pistachio)
¼ tsp jaiphal (nutmeg), ¼ tsp javetri (mace), ½ tbsp kachri powder

### BASTING (POURING ON THE SEEKHS)

2 tbsp melted butter or oil

1. Wash the mince in a strainer and squeeze out all the excess water by pressing well. Grind the mince twice till smooth.
2. Roast magaz and chironji on a hot tawa. Cool.

16

3. Grind ginger, garlic, green chillies, coriander, kaju, badam, kishmish, pista, jaiphal, javetri, kachri and roasted chironji and magaz in a grinder. Remove from grinder to a big bowl.

4. Add bread crumbs, oil, cornflour, garam masala, salt and chicken mince. Mix well and marinate covered in the refrigerator for 4-5 hours or till serving time.

5. At serving time, heat an electric oven at 180°C or gas tandoor on moderate heat.

6. Grease a skewer and warm it a little on fire. Take a big ball of the mince mixture and hold the skewer carefully in the other hand. Press the mince on to the skewer very carefully. The mince will immediately stick to the slightly hot skewer. If the skewers are very cold the mince will not stick. Make one big seekh on the skewer. Repeat with the left over mince on all the other skewers.

7. Place the skewers in the hot oven or gas tandoor. Cook for 10-15 minutes or till done, rotating the skewers. When the seekhs get cooked, gently remove the kebab from the skewers with the help of a cloth. Cut each into 1" pieces to serve.

# *Achaari Paneer Tikka*

*Pickle flavoured masala paneer tikka.*

*Picture on facing page*      Makes 16

400 gms paneer - cut into 1½" rectangles of ¾" thickness
2 tsp ginger-garlic paste, 1 tsp cornflour
1 cup curd - hang in a muslin cloth for ½ hour, 2 tbsp oil
½ tsp haldi (turmeric) powder, 1 tsp amchoor (dried mango powder)
1 tsp dhania powder, ½ tsp garam masala, 1 tsp salt or to taste, ½ tsp sugar
1 onion - chopped finely, 2 green chillies - chopped
some chaat masala to sprinkle

### ACHAARI MASALA

1 tbsp saunf (aniseeds), ½ tsp sarson (mustard seeds), ½ tsp kalonji (onion seeds), a pinch of methi daana (fenugreek seeds), ½ tsp jeera (cumin seeds)

1. Cut paneer into 1½" rectangles, of about ¾" thickness.
2. Collect seeds of achaari masala- saunf, sarson, methi daana, kalonji and jeera together.      *contd...*

3. Heat 2 tbsp oil. Add the collected seeds together to the hot oil. Let saunf change colour.
4. Add onions and chopped green chillies. Cook till onions turn golden brown.
5. Reduce heat. Add haldi, amchoor, dhania powder, garam masala, salt and sugar. Mix. Remove from fire. Transfer to a plate to cool.
6. Beat curd till smooth. Add garlic-ginger paste and cornflour. Add the onion masala also to the curd.
7. Add the paneer cubes to the curd. Marinate till serving time.
8. At serving time, rub oil generously over the grill of the oven or wire rack of a gas tandoor. Place paneer on the greased wire rack or grill of the oven.
9. Heat an oven to 180°C or a gas tandoor on moderate flame. Grill paneer for 15 minutes. Spoon some oil or melted butter on the paneer pieces in the oven or tandoor and grill further for 5 minutes.
10. Serve hot sprinkled with chaat masala.

**Tip:** To cook the tikkas in the oven, place a drip tray under the wire rack on which the tikkas are placed, to collect the drippings.

# *Akbari Kebabs*

*Chicken breasts stuffed with a spiced cheese filling.*

*Serves 4*

2 chicken breasts (300gm)

## IST MARINADE
1 tbsp lemon juice, ½ tsp salt, ½ tsp red chilli powder

## 2ND MARINADE
1 cup thick curd - hang for 15-20 minutes
¼ cup thick cream
2 tbsp grated cheese
1 tsp shah jeera (black cumin) - roughly crushed
1 tbsp cornflour
1 tsp red chilli powder, 1 tsp salt, a pinch of haldi, 1 tsp garam masala
1 tbsp ginger-garlic paste
1 tbsp barbecue masala or tandoori masala (optional)
2 tbsp coriander - chopped

## FILLING
1 onion - cut into rings & then cut rings into half
1 tbsp coriander - chopped
1 tsp shah jeera (black cumin or caraway seeds)
100 gm cheese - finely grated
1½ tbsp oil
1 tsp ginger-garlic paste
1 tbsp coriander

1. Open the breast slices to get thin big pieces (you can ask your butcher to do it for you). Cut each breast into 4 long strips, about 1½" wide to make rolls.
2. Wash and pat dry the chicken strips.
3. Marinate the chicken with the first marinade – salt, lemon juice and chilli powder.
4. Mix the ingredients of the 2nd marinade together in a bowl.
5. Pick up the chicken pieces from the lemon juice marinade and squeeze gently. Put them in the curd-cream marinade in the bowl.

6. For the filling, heat oil. Add shah jeera. Let it change colour. Add onion. Cook till onion turns soft. Add ginger-garlic paste and coriander. Cook for 1 minute. Remove from fire. Add cheese.

7. To make the kebab, take a strip of chicken. Place 1 tbsp of filling on one end of the chicken strip and roll it forward tightly to form a roll. Place the roll on the greased wire rack. Pat the remaining marinade on the rolls.

8. Heat a gas tandoor or an oven to 180°C. Grill for ½ hour, turning and basting with melted butter or oil after 20 minutes. Cook till tender.

**Tip:**
- The kebabs should always be placed on a wire rack or grill and never on a tray when you put them in the oven. When they are in the oven, some liquid tends to drip which collects around the kebabs which makes them soggy, if they are placed on a tray. If they are on a wire mesh or rack, the liquid falls down and the kebabs remain dry and hence turn crisp on the outside.

# *Galouti Kebab*

*Delicious kebabs which melt in your mouth! Must give it a try.*

*Makes 15 kebabs*

## PRESSURE COOK TOGETHER

500 gm keema (lamb mince)
½ tsp garam masala, ¼ tsp jaiphal (nutmeg) powder, ¼ tsp javetri (mace)
seeds of 3 moti illaichi, 2" stick dalchini (cinnamon)

## OTHER INGREDIENTS

1½ tbsp kachri powder, ¼ tsp mitha soda (soda-bi-carb)
2 onions - cut into slices, 2 tbsp ginger-garlic paste
1 egg white - seperate egg yolk from egg white, 4 tbsp besan (gram flour)
2 tbsp chopped coriander
1 tsp tandoori masala, ½ tsp garam masala, ½ tsp red chilli powder
1 tsp salt or to taste, 5 tbsp melted butter, oil for frying

## BATTER

1 egg, 2 tsp maida (plain flour)

1. Wash the mince in a strainer and press out excess water.
2. Put the mince in a cooker. Add ¼ tsp jaiphal, ¼ tsp javetri, seeds of 3 moti illachi, 1" stick dalchini and 4 cups water. Give 5-6 whistles. Remove from fire. The keema should be cooked. After the pressure drops, if there is any water, dry out the water completely on fire.
3. Place boiled mince in a mixer blender. Churn till smooth. Keep aside.
4. Heat 1 cup oil in a kadhai and fry the sliced onions till golden brown. Remove from oil with a slotted spoon and grind to a brown paste.
5. Add the brown onion paste, ginger-garlic paste, kachri powder, egg white, salt, chilli powder, tandoori masala, butter & garam masala to the mince mixture. Mix to get a sticky consistency. Remove to a bowl.
6. Roast besan in a kadhai or pan on low heat till light golden and fragrant.
7. Add roasted besan and chopped coriander to the mince mixture. Keep for 1 hour in the refrigerator. Shape mince into flat, 4" diameter tikkis.
8. Beat 1 egg and add 1 tsp maida to it. Dip the tikkis into the egg batter.
9. Shallow fry on low heat in 4 tbsp oil on a tawa or pan, till brown on both sides. Sprinkle some chaat masala and serve with onion rings mixed with some lemon juice and salt. Serve hot.

# *Poodina Kaju Kebabs*

*Cashew kebabs stuffed with a minty filling.*

*Serves 6-8*

2 big potatoes - chopped, 2 small onions - chopped

¾ cup shelled peas

½ of a small cauliflower - cut into small florets

4 slices of bread - broken into pieces and ground in a mixer to get fresh crumbs

1" piece ginger - crushed, 5-6 flakes garlic - crushed (2 tsp ginger-garlic paste)

½ tsp red chilli powder

½ tsp garam masala

2 tsp tomato sauce

1½ tsp salt or to taste

1 green chilli - finely chopped

2 tbsp chopped fresh coriander

15 cashewnuts - ground to a coarse powder in a small spice grinder

4 tbsp cornflour

**FILLING**
2-3 tbsp very finely chopped poodina(mint)
½ small onion - chopped finely, ¼ tsp amchoor
¼ tsp salt

1. Pressure cook potatoes, cauliflower, onion and peas with 1 cup water to give one whistle. Keep on fire for 5 minutes. Remove from fire. Cool. Drain & leave in a sieve for about 5 minutes to remove excess water.
2. Mash the vegetables and add ginger, garlic, red chilli powder, garam masala, salt and tomato sauce.
3. Add green chilli, fresh coriander, cashewnuts and cornflour and fresh bread crumbs.
4. Mix all ingredients of the filling together. Keep aside.
5. Break off small balls of the vegetable mixture and pat them into flat circular shapes about ½" thick, with wet hands.
6. Stuff a little of the filling and form a ball. Shape again into a flat disc.
7. Heat 4-5 tbsp oil in a frying pan or on a tawa and fry gently over medium heat, turning once.
8. Remove on a paper napkin to remove excess oil.

# Pista Murg Tikka

*Cubes of chicken marinated with pistachio paste and hung curd.*

### Serves 6

500 gm boneless chicken - cut into 2" pieces

**MARINADE**

4 tbsp pista - soaked in warm water, peeled and ground to a green paste
with 2 tbsp water
1 cup dahi (yogurt) - hang for ½ hour in a muslin cloth
1 tbsp ginger paste
1 tbsp garlic paste
½ tsp garam masala
½ tsp shah jeera (black cumin)
1 tsp red chilli powder
3 tbsp cornflour
3 tbsp oil
1 tsp salt

**BASTING (POURING ON THE KEBABS)**
3 tbsp oil

**GARNISH**
a pinch of kesar (saffron) - soaked in 1 tbsp milk
1 tsp pistas - chopped

1. Mix all the ingredients of the marinade and put the tikkas in it. Keep aside for 4-5 hours in the refrigerator.
2. Heat an electric oven at 180°C or a gas tandoor on moderate heat.
3. Oil the wire rack of the oven. Place the tikkas on it, leaving behind the extra marinade. Keep the left over marinade aside.
4. Grill for 10 minutes. Spoon some oil on the tikkas and grill for another 5 minutes. Transfer to a serving platter.
5. On a slow fire heat the leftover marinade. When it begins to thicken, add the saffron soaked in milk and cook for 1-2 minutes. Pour over the tikkas.
6. Sprinkle with chopped pistas and serve with hari chutney.

# Subz Kakori

*Very soft and delicious vegetarian seekh kebabs.*

## Serves 4-5

3 potatoes (medium) - boiled
(250 gm) 2 cups jimikand (yam) - chopped and boiled
½ cup crumbled paneer, 4 tbsp cashewnuts - ground
1 tsp ginger paste, 1 tsp garlic paste, 1 cup onion - very finely chopped
2 green chillies - very finely chopped
2 tbsp green coriander - very finely chopped
1 tsp bhuna jeera (cumin roasted), 1 tsp red chilli powder, ¼ tsp amchoor
2 bread slices - crumbled in a grinder to get fresh crumbs
1½ tsp salt, or to taste, a pinch of tandoori red colour

## BASTING
2 tbsp melted butter or oil

## GARNISH
tandoori khatta masala or chaat masala

1. Boil the potatoes. Peel and mash.
2. Pressure cook chopped yam with ½ cup water and ½ tsp salt to give 3 whistles. Remove from fire. After the pressure drops, keep it on fire to dry, if there is any excess water. Mash it to a paste.
3. Mix mashed potatoes, yam and all other ingredients, making a slightly stiff dough.
4. Oil and wipe the skewers. Heat the tandoor or oven. Press into sausage-shaped kababs on the skewers and cook for about 5 minutes in a hot tandoor or grill. Pour some melted butter on the kebabs to baste them when they get half done. Turn side and grill for 5-7 minutes or till golden brown. If you do not wish to grill the kebabs, shallow fry in 2 tbsp oil in a pan, turning sides till browned evenly.
5. Sprinkle some tandoori or chaat masala and serve with onion rings and lemon wedges.

**Note:** Turn kebabs only after they are half done, otherwise they tend to break.

# Shami Kebab

*Makes 15 kebabs*

**PRESSURE COOK TOGETHER**

½ kg mutton mince (keema)

¼ cup channa dal - soaked in warm water for 20-30 minutes and drained

1 onion - sliced

10 flakes garlic - chopped, 2" piece ginger - chopped

2 tsp saboot dhania (coriander seeds)

1 tsp jeera (cumin seeds), 3-4 laung (cloves)

seeds of 2 chhoti illaichi (green cardamoms)

seeds of 2 moti illaichi (brown cardamoms)

½" stick dalchini (cinnamon), 1 tej patta (bay leaf)

4-5 saboot kali mirch (peppercorns)

2-3 dry, whole red chillies

salt to taste

½ cup water

### MINTY FILING (MIX TOGETHER)
1 onion - very finely chopped
1 tbsp chopped poodina(mint), 1 tbsp chopped hara dhania
2 green chillies - finely chopped, a big pinch of salt

1. Wash the mince in a strainer and press well to drain out the water well through the strainer.
2. Add all the ingredients to the mince & pressure cook to give 2 whistles. Keep on low flame for 2 minutes. Remove from fire.
3. When the pressure drops, uncover the pressure cooker. If there is any water left, keep the cooker on fire to dry the water. (If the mince is wet, the kebabs will break while frying).
4. Dry grind the well dried minced meat either on a stone grinder or in a mixer till smooth without adding any water while grinding. (Discard bay leaf).
5. To prepare kebabs, make 2 tiny balls. Flatten both and sandwich them together with a teaspoon of the filling. Press gently to stick together.
6. Shallow fry in a little oil in a non stick tawa on medium heat, till brown. Serve hot.

# Dil Bahar-e-Murg/Gosht
## (Chicken & Mutton Main dishes)

# Murg Nizam

*A semi-dry chicken `masala' cooked with nuts (cashewnuts, peanuts and coconut) and sesame seeds.*

Serves 6-7        Picture on page 37

800 gm chicken - cut into 8-12 pieces
¼ cup kaju (cashewnuts)
8 tbsp oil or ghee
2 onions - chopped
3 tbsp ginger paste, 3 tbsp garlic paste
8 green chillies - slit, deseeded & chopped
1 tsp haldi (turmeric powder)
2½ tsp salt, or to taste
¼ cup peanuts & 2 tbsp til (sesame seeds) - pounded together (crushed coarsely)
½ cup coconut - brown skin removed & grated
¾ cup dahi (yogurt) - whipped till smooth

1 tsp garam masala
1 tbsp lemon juice
½ cup chopped green coriander
¼ cup chopped poodina (mint)

1. Heat oil and fry cashewnuts until golden brown. Remove from oil and keep aside.
2. Heat the left over oil again and add onions and saute over medium heat until golden brown.
3. Add the ginger and garlic pastes, stir for a minute.
4. Add green chillies, salt and turmeric. Mix.
5. Add the pounded peanuts and sesame seeds and grated coconut, stir for a minute.
6. Reduce heat. Add yoghurt and bhuno for 3-4 minutes.
7. Add chicken, bhuno for 5-10 minutes. Add about 1½ cups water, boil, simmer for 10-15 minutes, or until tender. Adjust the seasoning.
8. Sprinkle garam masala, lemon juice, coriander, mint and fried cashewnuts. Remove to a dish and serve with nan or parantha.

*Murg Nizam : Recipe on page 35*  ➤

# Gosht Khada Masala

*Delicious mutton, quite different from the regular taste of mutton.*

*Serves 6-8*

1 kg mutton (boneless)
1½ cups yogurt - beat well till smooth
¾ cup oil
3 onions - chopped
5 tbsp garlic - chopped, 5 tbsp ginger - chopped
5 green chillies - chopped
4 tomatoes - chopped

**KHADA MASALAS (WHOLE SPICES)**
2 moti illaichi (black cardamom)
5 laung (cloves)
¼ tsp javetri (mace)
5 chhoti illaichi (green cardamom)
1" stick dalchini (cinnamon), 1 bay leaf (tej patta)

## CRUSH SPICES TOGETHER
2 tsp saboot dhania (coriander seeds)
12 saboot kali mirch (peppercorns)
4 whole dry, red chillies
1 tsp shah jeera (black cumin)

1. Heat oil in a pressure cooker, add all the khada masalas. Let them crackle, for about a minute.
2. Add onions. Cook till golden brown.
3. Add garlic, ginger, and green chilles. Stir for a minute.
4. Add mutton and the crushed spices. Bhuno till the mutton pieces are brown.
5. Reduce heat. Add yogurt and bhuno till masala leaves the oil.
6. Add 2 cups water and pressure cook for 7 minutes after the first whistle and then keep on low heat for 5 minutes.
7. Serve sprinkled with garam masala and coriander.

# *Makhani Murg* (Butter Chicken)

### *Serves 4*

1 chicken (750 gm) - cut into 8 pieces

## MARINADE FOR TANDOORI MURG

1 cup thick curd - hang in a muslin cloth for ½ hour
2 tbsp maida, 3 tsp ginger-garlic paste, a pinch of orange red colour
½ tsp jeera powder, ½ tsp dhania powder, 2 tbsp oil
½ tsp garam masala powder, 1 tsp tandoori masala, 1½ tsp amchoor powder
1½ tsp salt, 1 tsp red chilli powder, 4 tbsp oil for basting (pouring)

## MAKHANI GRAVY

2 tbsp butter, 2-3 tbsp oil, 1 tej patta (bay leaf), 2 tbsp ginger-garlic paste
½ kg (6-7) tomatoes - blended to a very smooth puree
2-3 tbsp cashewnuts - soaked in hot water for 15 minutes, drained and ground to
a very fine paste with a little water
¼ tsp kashmiri or degi mirch
1 cup milk, 2 tbsp cream
½ tsp garam masala, 1 tsp tandoori masala, ¼ tsp sugar or to taste

1. Mix all ingredients of the marinade. Marinate chicken in it for 2 hours.
2. Rub the grill with oil and place the marinated chicken on it. Grill for 8-10 minutes in an oven at 180°C. Overturn again, baste (pour) with oil & grill for another 10-12 minutes or till tender and crisp.Keep aside.
3. For the makhani gravy, heat butter and oil together in a kadhai. Add tej patta. Stir for a few seconds. Add ginger and garlic paste, cook until liquid evaporates and paste just changes colour.
4. Add pureed tomatoes, degi mirch and sugar. Cook until the puree turns very dry and fat separates.
5. Add cashew paste, stir for a few seconds on medium heat till fat separates. Remove from fire. Add milk and about ½ cup of water to get the desired gravy. Return to fire. Boil on low heat, stirring constantly.
6. Add chicken. Simmer for 5-7 minutes till the gravy turns to a bright colour. Remove from fire and stir in cream, stirring continuously. Add garam masala, tandoori masala and salt. Stir. Remove from fire. Garnish with 1 tbsp of cream and slit green chillies.

**Note:** To prepare tandoori chicken, if you do not have a tandoor or an oven, simply marinate the chicken and cook in a kadhai till crisp.

# Haryali Chicken

*The addition of fresh methi to spinach makes the dish tastier.*

### Serves 6-8

1 chicken (700-800 gm) - cut into 12 pieces
500 gm paalak (spinach)
250 gm methi (fenugreek greens)
2-3 onions - chopped finely
3 tbsp ginger-garlic-green chilli paste
1 large tomato - chopped
½ cup thick curd - beat well till smooth
1 tsp garam masala
1 tsp chilli powder
salt to taste
½ cup milk or water
4-5 tbsp oil
3 tbsp cream (optional)

1. Discard stems of spinach and chop the leaves finely. Wash leaves in plenty of water, changing water several times.
2. Wash the methi leaves in the same way. Sprinkle little salt and squeeze to remove bitterness from the leaves. Keep aside.
3. Heat oil in a heavy bottomed pan. Add onions. Cook till light brown.
4. Add the ginger-garlic paste. Cook for 1 minute.
5. Add tomato. Cook for 1 minute, till it turns mushy. Add curd, salt, chilli powder, garam masala and cook on high flame or till oil separates a little.
6. Squeeze out all the excess water from spinach and methi leaves. Add to the masala. Cook on high flame till all the excess water evaporates.
7. Now add the washed chicken pieces and bhuno or stir fry on high flame stirring constantly.
8. Cook till water evaporates and the masala sticks to the chicken pieces.
9. Add milk or water. Reduce heat. Cover and cook till chicken is tender.
10. Remove cover and again cook for 2 to 3 minutes on low heat or till chicken pieces are coated with spinach masala.
11. Add cream, stir well and cook for ½ a minute. Remove. Serve hot.

# Shahi Kaju Murg

*A nawaabi dish — rich cashew gravy flavoured with shah jeera and chhoti illaichi.*

Picture on back cover                Serves 6-8

1 chicken (700-800 gm) - cut into 12 pieces

**MARINADE**

2-3 tbsp ginger-garlic paste

¾ cup thick curd

½ tsp chilli powder, salt to taste, 1 tsp garam masala

**OTHER INGREDIENTS**

4-5 tbsp oil

1 tej patta (bay leaf), ½ tsp shah jeera (black cumin)

2-3 chhoti illaichi (green cardamoms) - pounded lightly

3 large onions - ground to a paste

¾ cup milk

3 tbsp cream

## GRIND TO A FINE PASTE
6 tbsp broken cashewnuts soaked in a 3-4 tbsp of hot water

1. Marinate the chicken with beaten curd, ginger-garlic paste, salt, garam masala and chilli powder.
2. Soak cashewnuts in 3-4 tbsp of hot water for 15 minutes. Grind to a smooth paste. Keep aside.
3. Heat oil in a pan. Add tej patta, chhoti illaichi and shah jeera. Wait for a few seconds.
4. Add the onions and cook stirring constantly, till light brown.
5. Stir in the chicken pieces alongwith the marinade. Cook on high flame for 5-7 minutes, stirring continously.
6. Add the cashewnut paste. Stir constantly on medium or high heat till the juices evaporate and oil separates.
7. Lower the heat and add milk and ½ cup water. Cover and cook till the chicken is tender and oil separates.
8. Add cream, stir well and cook for ½ a minute. Remove. Serve sprinkled with some garam masala and chopped coriander leaves.

# *Shahjehani Gosht*

*Rich, brown lamb dish, marinated in a spiced marinade.*

*Picture on pacing page*         *Serves 4*

600 gm boneless lamb - trimmed and cubed
¾ cup oil
4 potatoes - boiled, peeled and cut into four pieces
3 large onions - peeled and cut into four pieces
8 laung (cloves)

**MARINADE**
1 cup dahi (yogurt)
2 tsp ginger paste, 2 tsp garlic paste
½ cup coriander leaves - chopped
10 tbsp tomato puree
1 tsp red chilli powder, 1 tsp haldi (turmeric powder)
2 tsp salt
1 tsp dalchini (cinnamon) powder

1. Mix all ingredients of the marinade in a pan. Add the meat and mix well. Marinate the meat in this mixture for 1 hour.
2. Heat oil in a karahi and stir-fry the potatoes until golden. Remove from oil and keep aside.
3. In the same oil stir-fry the onions until golden. Remove from oil and keep aside.
4. Transfer the remaing hot oil to a pressure cooker. Add laung. Wait for a minute and then add the meat mixture and stir. Bhuno well for 10 minutes till dahi dries up. Bhuno the meat further for 5-7 minutes.
5. Add 3 cups water and pressure cook for 7 minutes after the first whistle and then keep on low heat for 5 minutes.
6. Remove from fire. After the pressure drops, open the cooker and add the fried potatoes and onions and cook for 5 more minutes.
7. Serve hot with nan or roti.

# Mutton Malai Kofta

*Minced meat balls, stuffed with dry fruits and cooked in a delicious creamy gravy.*

### Makes 15

**KOFTA**

500 gm keema (minced meat)
4 tbsp oil
1 onion - finely chopped
8 finely chopped flakes of garlic
1 tbsp grated ginger
2 green chillies - finely chopped
½ tsp red chilli powder
1½ tsp salt
1 egg and 1 yolk
¼ tsp garam masala

*contd...*

## FILLING
15 pistachio (pistas)
15 sultanas (kishmish)
15 almonds (badam)

## GRAVY
4 tbsp oil
2 onions - grated
1 tsp finely chopped garlic, 1 tbsp ginger paste
½ tsp red chilli powder
1½ tbsp dhania powder
1 tsp salt
3 large tomatoes - blanched, peeled and chopped
2½ cups water or stock
½ cup cream
1 tbsp finely chopped fresh coriander leaves

1. Heat 4 tbsp oil, fry the finely chopped onions & garlic till golden brown.
2. Add minced meat, ginger, green chillies, red chilli powder and salt.

Mix well. Cook covered on slow fire for 5-7 minutes till the juices dry up. Remove from the fire. Cool. Grind to a paste.

3. Beat eggs and mix with the mince. Add ½ tsp garam masala too.
4. Divide mince mixture into 15 equal parts. Flatten each part of the mince, put on it's centre 1 pista, 1 almond and 1 kishmish. With the help of a little water shape it into a round ball of the size of walnut and fry in hot oil till golden in colour.
5. To prepare the gravy, heat 4 tbsp oil and fry the onions and the garlic till golden brown. Add red chilli powder, dhania powder and salt. Add ginger and mix.
6. Add tomatoes. Bhuno well for 5-7 minutes till the tomatoes blend well.
7. Add water or stock and simmer on slow fire for about 15 minutes.
8. Add the fried koftas to the gravy. Allow them to simmer for 10 minutes or till they are soft and swollen and the gravy is reduced to half. Keep aside till serving time.
9. At serving time, heat the koftas in gravy and reduce heat. Pour in the cream and mix. Remove from fire. Transfer to a serving dish. Sprinkle ¼ tsp garam masala and finely chopped coriander leaves.

# Achaari Korma

Picture on page 1          Serves 6-8

1 kg mutton (boneless spring lamb)
½ tsp haldi (turmeric)
1 tsp salt or to taste
4 tsp mustard oil
3 tbsp ghee
2 onions - sliced
8 whole red chillies, 1 tsp red chilli powder
2 tsp garlic - chopped, 2 tsp ginger chopped
1 cup yogurt - whipped till smooth
2 tbsp lemon juice
2 tbsp gur (jaggery) - grated

## ACHAARI MASALA

1 tbsp saunf (aniseeds), ½ tsp sarson (mustard seeds), 1 tsp kalonji (onion seeds), ½ tsp methi daana (fenugreek seeds), 1 tsp jeera (cumin seeds)
5 laung (cloves), a pinch of asafoetida (*hing*)

1. In a pressure cooker put mutton, haldi, ½ tsp salt and 6 cups water and pressure cook for 7 minutes after the first whistle and then keep on low heat for 10 minutes. After pressure drops, drain & keep the stock aside.
2. Heat mustard oil in karahi to a smoking point, reduce to medium heat and add ghee.
3. When the ghee becomes hot, add onion slices and fry till golden brown. Remove the onions and keep aside a little for garnishing.
4. In the same ghee add whole red chillies and fry until black. Remove and discard the chillies.
5. Reheat this chilli oil, add jeera, methi daana, kalunji, saunf, sarson, laung and hing. Saute till jeera begins to change colour.
6. Add the fried onions, red chilli powder, ginger, garlic, gur and the boiled mutton. Bhuno for 5-10 minutes till the mutton becomes brownish in color.
7. Add the reserved stock and lemon juice, simmer for 2-3 minutes
8. Add the yogurt & mix well. Cook till oil separates. Adjust the seasoning.
9. Remove from the fire. Add yogurt. Cook on slow flame for a minute.
10. Serve garnished with the remaining fried onions and serve with nan.

# *Shahi Meat*

*A royal, lamb curry.*

*Serves 4*

600 gm lean lamb - cubed
1 tsp haldi (turmeric powder), 1 tsp dhania (coriander powder)
½ tsp salt to taste
6 tbsp oil
2 onions - chopped finely
1-2 green chillies - chopped finely
1½ cups dahi (yogurt) - beat till smooth
4 tbsp coriander leaves - chopped

## GRIND TOGETHER TO A ROUGH PASTE
1 tsp jeera (cumin seeds)
1 tsp kali sarson (black mustard seeds)
2 tsp khus khus (poppy seeds)
2 tsp anardana (pomegranate seeds)
1" piece ginger, 10-12 flakes garlic

1. Marinate the lamb with haldi, dhania powder and **salt** for 15 minutes.
2. Grind the jeera, sarson, khus khus and anaar dana with ginger and garlic and a little water to make a coarse paste.
3. Heat 6 tbsp oil in a heavy bottomed kadhai and add the onions. Fry until golden and add the green chillies.
4. Add the above paste. Fry for a minute and add the lamb. Bhuno, stirring continuously on medium heat for about 10 minutes, till it turns brown on all sides and oil separates. Do not add any water even if the mutton sticks to the bottom of the kadhai. Keep stirring nicely.
5. Add the well beaten yogurt and enough water to make a thick gravy. Add ½ tsp salt or to taste. Boil.
6. Add 2 cups water and pressure cook for 7 minutes after the first whistle and then keep on low heat for 5 minutes.
7. Serve hot, sprinkled with coriander.

# *Piste Waala Murg*

*A rich Mughlai style of cooking chicken with pista paste, giving the curry a lovely green colour and flavour.*

Picture on cover          *Serves 6*

1 small chicken - cut into 12 pieces

or

500 gm boneless chicken, cut into 1½" pieces

2 large onions

½ cup yogurt - beat well till smooth

2 tsp ginger-garlic paste or 1" ginger piece & 4-5 flakes garlic - crushed to a paste

4 tbsp oil

2 tbsp coriander powder

1 tsp white pepper powder

2 tsp salt, or to taste

½ cup fresh cream

½ tsp garam masala powder

### GRIND TOGETHER TO A PASTE
½ cup pistas (pistachio nuts) - soaked in water and peeled
4 green chillies - finely chopped
¼ cup chopped fresh coriander

1. Peel and cut onions into 4 pieces. Boil in 1 cup water for 2-3 minutes. Drain, cool slightly and grind to a fine paste. Keep boiled onion paste aside.
2. Soak pistachio nuts in hot water for 10 minutes, drain and peel. Reserve a few peeled pistachio nuts for garnish.
3. Grind the remaining peeled pistachio nuts with chopped green chillies and coriander to a fine green paste with a little water.
4. Heat 4 tbsp oil in a pan, add boiled onion paste and saute for 4-5 minutes on low heat till dry and oil separates. See that the colour of the onions does not change to brown.
5. Add ginger-garlic paste and stir-fry for a minute.
6. Add coriander powder, white pepper powder and salt and mix well.
7. Stir in the pistachio and green chilli paste and cook for 2 minutes on low heat.

*contd...*

8. Add chicken pieces and saute for 4-5 minutes on moderate heat stirring continously.
9. Add 2 cups water and simmer covered on low heat for 15-20 minutes or until the chicken is completely cooked.
10. Reduce heat. Stir in yogurt & continue to simmer for 2 minutes, stirring continuously.
11. Stir in fresh cream, sprinkle garam masala powder and transfer to a serving dish.
12. Sprinkle remaining pistachio nuts and some cream.
13. Serve hot with parantha.

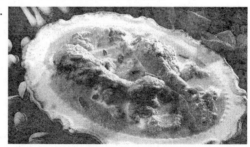

# Gulbahaar-e-Subz (Vegetables)

# Methi Malai Khumb Matar

*Picture on page 65*  *Serves 4-5*

200 gms mushrooms - preferably small in size
1 cup shelled, boiled or frozen peas
4 tbsp kasoori methi (dry fenugreek leaves)
1 tsp ginger-garlic paste, 1 tbsp butter, 3 tbsp oil
2 onions - ground to a paste
¼ cup malai (milk topping) - mix with ¼ cup milk and blend in a mixer for a few
seconds till smooth or ½ cup thin fresh cream
1 tsp salt or to taste, ½ tsp red chilli powder
½ tsp garam masala, a pinch of amchoor
½ cup milk (approx.)

**GRIND TOGETHER**
½ stick dalchini (cinnamon)
seeds of 2-3 chhoti illaichi (green cardamom)
3-4 laung (cloves), 4-5 saboot kali mirch (peppercorns)
2 tbsp kaju (cashewnuts)

1. Trim the stem of each mushroom. Leave them whole if small or cut them into 2 pieces, if big. Heat 1 tbsp butter in a kadhai and add the mushrooms. Stir fry on high flame till dry and golden. Add 1 tsp ginger-garlic paste, ½ tsp salt and a pinch of white or black pepper. Stir for 1 more minute and remove from fire. Keep cooked mushrooms aside.
2. Grind together dalchini, seeds of chhoti illaichi, laung, kali mirch and cashew to a powder in a small mixer grinder.
3. Heat 3 tbsp oil. Add onion paste and cook on low heat till oil separates. Do not let the onions turn brown.
4. Add the freshly ground masala-cashew powder. Cook for a few seconds.
5. Add the kasoori methi and malai, cook on low heat for 2-3 minutes till malai dries up.
6. Add salt, red chilli powder, garam masala & amchoor. Stir for 1 minute.
7. Add the boiled peas and mushrooms.
8. Add ½ cup milk to get a thick gravy. Add ½ cup water if the gravy appears too thick. Boil for 2-3 minutes. Serve.

# *Shahi Baby Corns*

*Baby corns in a red shahi gravy. If baby corns are not available, regular corn on the cob can be used instead.*

### *Serves 8*

200 gm baby corns or 2 small tender bhutte (corn on the cobs)
½-1 cup milk, approx.
2 tbsp kaju (cashews) - soaked for 10 minutes and ground to a paste with ¼ cup water

### GRIND TO A PASTE TOGETHER
2 small onions, 4 tomatoes, 1" piece ginger, 1 green chilli

### OTHER INGREDIENTS FOR GRAVY
4 tbsp oil, ½ tsp shah jeera
1 tsp dhania (coriander) powder, ½ tsp amchoor, 1½ tsp salt
½ tsp red chilli powder, 1 tsp garam masala
1 tsp tandoori masala
2-3 chhoti illaichi (green cardamom) - seeds crushed

### BAGHAR OR TEMPERING
1 tbsp oil, ½ tsp shah jeera (black cumin)
1 tsp finely chopped ginger
5-6 almonds (badaam) - cut into thin long pieces
¼ tsp red chilli powder

1. Choose small baby corns or thin tender bhuttas. Keep baby corns whole or cut each bhutta into 4 small pieces. If thick, slit each piece into two.
2. Put all the pieces of baby corns and ½ cup milk in a pan. Give one boil and keep on low heat for 2 minutes. If using bhuttas, use a pressure cooker to cook them. Pressure cook bhutta pieces with 1 cup milk to give one whistle. Then keep on low flame for 5 minutes. Remove from fire.
3. Grind onions, tomatoes, green chilli and ginger to a paste in a grinder.
4. Heat oil. Add shah jeera. After a minute, add onion-tomato paste and cook till dry and oil separates. Reduce flame. Add red chilli powder, dhania, amchoor, salt and garam masala. Cook for 1 minute.

*contd...*

5. Add cashew paste. Stir to mix well.
6. Keeping the flame low, add the left over milk from the boiled bhuttas, stirring continuously. Stir for 2-3 minutes.
7. Add corn and simmer on low flame for 3 minutes. Add enough (2-3 cups approx.) water to get a thin gravy. Boil. Simmer for 5-7 minutes till slightly thick. Add tandoori masala, chhoti illaichi, paneer and coriander.
8. Transfer to a serving dish.
9. Heat oil for baghar. Add jeera and ginger. After a few seconds, add almonds and stir. Add red chilli powder, remove from fire and pour the tempered oil on the gravy.

*Methi Malai Khumb Matar : Recipe on page 60* ➤

# *Safed Mughlai Paneer*

*Paneer in a rich, white curry.*

*Serves 4*

200 gm paneer - cut into ½" cubes
1 onion - grated
4 tbsp curd
1 cup (200 gm) fresh cream
1½ tbsp desi ghee or butter
¾ tsp garam masala
¾ tsp red chilli powder
¾ tsp salt or to taste
seeds of 3 chhoti illaichi (green cardamoms) - crushed

**SOAK IN ¼ CUP HOT WATER FOR 30 MINUTES**
1 tbsp khus-khus (poppy seeds)
1 tbsp kaju (cashewnuts)
1 tbsp magaz (melon seeds)

1. Soak khus khus, kaju and magaz in ¼ cup hot water for 30 minutes. Grind to a very fine paste.
2. Beat curd till very smooth.
3. Heat ghee. Add grated onion. Cook on low flame till it turns transparent and ghee separates. Do not let it turn brown by keeping on high flame.
4. Add kaju - khus paste. Cook for 2 minutes on low flame.
5. Gradually, add well beaten curd, stirring continuously. Cook for 5-7 minutes, stirring continuously on low flame.
6. Add garam masala, red chilli powder and salt.
7. Add cream. Stir. Add paneer cubes. Mix well. Add a little milk if you want to thin down the gravy.
8. At the time of serving, add powdered chhoti illaichi and heat till paneer turns soft.
9. Serve garnished with a swirl of cream and a small stalk of fresh coriander leaves arranged on any side of the dish.

# Dal Makhani

*An all time favourite.*

*Serves 6*

1 cup urad saboot (whole black beans)
2 tbsp chane ki dal (split gram dal)
2 tbsp rajmah (kidney beans) - soaked for 5-6 hours (optional)
4 tbsp ghee or oil
5 cups of water, 1½ tsp salt
1" piece ginger, 4 flakes garlic (optional)
2 dry red chillies
6 tomatoes - pureed in a grinder
½ cup cream
2 tsp dhania (coriander) powder
½ tsp garam masala (mixed spices)
¼ tsp grated jaiphal (nutmeg)
2 tbsp butter

1. Grind ginger, garlic and dry red chillies together to a paste.
2. Clean, wash dals. Pressure cook both dals and the soaked rajmah with 1 tbsp ghee, water, salt and half of the ginger-garlic paste. Keep the left over paste aside.
3. After the first whistle, keep on low flame for 40 minutes. Remove from fire. Keep aside.
4. Heat 3 tbsp ghee. Add tomatoes pureed in a grinder. Cook until ghee separates and it turns dry and thick.
5. Add the left over ginger paste, garam masala and coriander pd. Cook for a few seconds.
6. Add this tomato mixture to the boiled dal. Add butter. Simmer on low flame for 8-10 minutes.
7. Add cream and jaiphal. Mix. Remove from fire.
8. Garnish with a bunch of uncut coriander leaves dipped in chilled water for 15 minutes. Arrange the leaves in the centre of the dish and make thin white rings of thick cream around the coriander, pouring it with a small spoon. Serve hot.

# *Haryali Kofta*

*Picture on page 75*                    *Serves 6*

## KOFTA

150 gm paneer - crumbled
250 gm paalak (spinach)
½ tsp salt, ¼ tsp red chilli powder
1 tbsp cornflour
2 slices bread - grind in a mixer to get fresh crumbs

## GRAVY

½ kg palak (spinach) - chopped
2 onions - grind to a paste
1" piece ginger & 3-4 flakes garlic - grind to a paste (2 tsp)
3 tomatoes - pureed in a mixer
¾ cup milk
½ tsp red chilli powder, ½ tsp salt or to taste, ¼ tsp pepper
3 tbsp oil, 1 tbsp ghee

1. To prepare koftas, remove stems of paalak leaves. Wash in plenty of water and pressure cook with ¼ cup water. Remove after the first whistle. Chop boiled paalak finely. Keep in a strainer for 10 minutes. Squeeze well. Mix paalak, paneer, bread crumbs, cornflour, red chilli powder and salt. Make balls. Roll in maida and deep fry one at a time in moderately hot oil. Keep koftas aside.
2. To prepare the gravy, pressure cook ½ kg paalak with ½ cup water to give one whistle. Keep on low flame for 4-5 minutes. Blend to a paste in a grinder.
3. Heat 3 tbsp oil. Add onion paste and stir fry till golden brown.
4. Add tomatoes. Cook till dry. Add chilli powder and ginger-garlic paste. Cook on low flame for 5-7 minutes till tomatoes look well fried and oil separates.
5. Remove from fire. Add milk, stirring constantly. Return to fire and stir on low heat till dry.
6. Add paalak. Add salt and pepper. Stir fry for 5-7 minutes till paalak looks well fried and turns thick. Add ghee. Remove from fire.
7. Add koftas at the time of serving and heat for 1-2 minutes.

# Gobhi Mussallam

*Picture on page 2*                    *Serves 8*

2 very small whole cauliflowers
4 tbsp oil
¼ cup boiled peas - to garnish

## GRIND TO A PASTE

2 small onions
4 tomatoes
1" piece ginger
1 green chilli

## MASALA

2 tbsp cashews - soaked in ¼ cup water for 10 minutes and ground to a paste
4 tbsp oil
½ tsp shah jeera
1 tsp dhania (coriander) powder
½ tsp amchoor

salt to taste
½ tsp red chilli powder
1 tsp garam masala
1 tsp tandoori masala
2-3 chhoti illaichi (green cardamom) - seeds crushed
50 gms paneer - grated (½ cup)
3 tbsp chopped coriander
½ cup milk

1. Remove stem of cauliflower. Boil 5-6 cups water with 2 tsp salt. Put the whole cauliflower in it and leave it covered in hot water for 10 minutes. Remove from water and wash. Wipe dry with a towel.

2. Heat 5-6 tbsp oil in a large kadhai. Put both cauliflowers with flower side in oil. Cover and cook on medium flame, stirring occasionally till the cauliflowers turn golden (and brown at some places) and get cooked. Remove from oil and keep aside.

3. To prepare masala, grind onions, tomatoes, green chilli and ginger to a paste.

*contd...*

4.  Heat oil. Add shah jeera. After a minute, add onion-tomato paste and cook till dry and oil separates. Reduce flame. Add red chilli powder, dhania, amchoor and garam masala. Cook for 1 minute.
5.  Add cashew paste. Stir to mix well.
6.  Reduce heat. Keeping the flame low, add milk stirring continuously. Stir for 2-3 minutes to get a thick masala. Add salt to taste.
7.  Insert a little masala inbetween the florets of the fried cauliflower. Insert from the backside also.
8.  To the remaining masala, add enough water to get a gravy. Boil. Simmer for 5-7 minutes till slightly thick. Add tandoori masala, chhoti illaichi, paneer and coriander. Boil. Add a little salt. Cook for 1 minute. Remove from fire.
9.  To serve, arrange the cauliflowers on a platter. Add 3-4 tbsp water to the masala to make it a little thin. Boil. Pour over the arranged cauliflowers. Heat in a preheated oven.
10. Sprinkle some boiled peas on it and on the sides. Serve.

*Haryali Kofta : Recipe on page 70* ➢
*Missi Roti : Recipe on page 93* ➢

# *Manzil-e-Paneer*

*A quick attractive way of serving paneer.*

### *Serves 8*

700-800 gm paneer - cut into a long, thick slab (7" long and 2" thick, approx.)
salt, pepper and chaat masala, 2-3 tbsp grated cheese

### FILLING (MIX TOGETHER)
½ cup grated carrot (½ carrot), ¼ cup grated cabbage, 4 tbsp grated cheese
¼ tsp salt and ¼ tsp freshly ground pepper, or to taste

### TOMATO SAUCE
5 large tomatoes - chopped roughly & boiled with ½ cup water
6 tbsp ready made tomato puree, 2 tbsp oil, 1 tsp crushed garlic (6-8 flakes)
½ tsp black pepper, ½ tsp salt and ¼ tsp pepper, or to taste, 3 tbsp cream

1.  To prepare the sauce, boil chopped tomatoes in ½ cup water. Keep on low heat for 4-5 minutes till soft. Remove from fire. Mash and strain. Discard the skin. Keep fresh tomato puree aside.
2.  Heat oil. Reduce heat. Add garlic and stir till it just starts to change colour. Do not make it brown.

3. Add 6 tbsp ready made tomato puree. Cook till oil separates, for about 2-3 minutes on medium flame.
4. Add the prepared fresh tomato puree and give one boil. Simmer on low heat for 5-6 minutes. Remove from fire. Cool to room temperature.
5. Mix in cream. Add salt and pepper to taste and keep the sauce aside.
6. Cut paneer into 3 equal pieces lengthwise. Sprinkle salt, pepper and chat masala on both sides of each slice of paneer. Saute each piece of paneer in 2 tbsp oil on a tawa, turning side till golden.
7. In a shallow rectangular serving dish, put ¼ of the prepared sauce.
8. Place a paneer slab on the sauce.
9. Spread ½ of the carrot-cabbage filling on it.
10. Press another piece of paneer on it.
11. Again put the filling on it. Cover with the last piece of paneer. Press.
12. Pour the sauce all over the paneer to cover the top and the sides completely. Grate cheese on top. Sprinkle some pepper.
13. If using a microwave, cover loosely with a cling film and micro high for 2 minutes. If using an ordinary oven, cover loosely with aluminium foil & heat for 8-10 minutes in a moderately hot oven at 180°C till hot.

# *Baghare Baingan*

*Baingan cooked with peanuts.*

### Serves 4

250 gm (8-10 pieces) brinjals (small, round variety)
1 tbsp roasted peanuts - crushed on a chakla
¾ tsp salt
½ tsp red chillies
¼ tsp garam masala
6-7 tbsp oil
1 big onion - finely grated
½ tsp saunf (fennel seeds) - crushed on a chakla
1 tsp full tamarind (a small marble sized ball of imli)
½ tsp shakkar or gur (powdered jaggery)
½" piece ginger - chopped
5-6 flakes garlic
1 tbsp fresh coriander leaves

### ROAST TOGETHER
2 tsp freshly grated or desiccated (powdered) coconut
2 tsp til (sesame seeds)
2 tsp saboot dhania (coriander seeds)
½ tsp jeera (cumin seeds)

1.  Wash and slit brinjals along the length from the side to form a pocket.
2.  Soak a small marble sized ball of tamarind in ¼ cup of warm water for a while. Rub to extract pulp and keep aside.
3.  Roast coconut, til, jeera and coriander seeds on a tawa on low flame for about 2 minutes, till they just change colour and become fragrant.
4.  Grind the roasted ingredients along with gur, ginger, garlic and coriander leaves with 2-3 tbsp water to a paste.
5.  Add salt, red chillies, garam masala and crushed peanuts to the paste. Mix well. Fill this into the brinjals.
6.  Heat 6-7 tbsp oil in a non stick pan or a large kadhai. Add brinjals, one by one, arranging in the pan or kadhai. Turn side after 2 minutes. Reduce heat and cover and cook on low heat, for about 15 minutes,

*contd...*

till they turn soft. Change sides once in between. Feel with a knife if the brinjals have turned soft. Remove from oil and keep aside. Remove all the masala also from the oil.

7. Heat the leftover oil and add crushed saunf. When it changes colour, add onion and cook to a light golden colour. Add ¼ tsp of salt and ¼ tsp red chilli powder.

8. Add tamarind juice. Mix. Add cooked brinjals, cover and keep for 5 minutes, on low heat, stirring occasionally taking care not to break the brinjals. Serve hot.

# Biryani & Rotis

# *Mutton Biryani*

*Delicious two coloured biryani. Impossible for the guests to ignore.*

*Picture on page 1*          *Serves 6*

3 cups basmati rice
½ kg mutton (champae)
8-10 flakes garlic- chopped, 4" piece ginger- chopped
1 tej patta (bay leaf), 4 laung (cloves), 5 saboot kali mirch (peppercorns)
1" stick dalchini (cinnamon), 2 moti illachi (black cardamoms)
4 chhoti illaichi (green cardamoms)
6 tbsp ghee or oil
1 onion - sliced
1 tsp red chilli powder, 3 tsp salt
1 tsp dhania powder, 1 tsp garam masla
¼ tsp orange colour, ½ tsp yellow colour
2 tsp kewra water (flavouring)

**COARSELY POWDER TOGETHER & TIE SPICES IN A MUSLIN CLOTH**
2 tsp saunf (aniseeds), 2 tsp saboot dhania (coriander seeds)
2 tsp jeera (cumin seeds)

1. Wash rice and preferably soak for 20 minutes.
2. Put mutton in a pressure cooker. Add 1 tsp salt, muslin spice bag, garlic, ginger, tej patta, laung, chhoti illaichi, moti illaichi and 9 cups of water. Give 2 whistles and cook on low heat till the mutton is tender. Remove from fire. Put the mutton in a strainer and strain. Keep the stock aside.
3. Heat oil in a kadhai. Add onion slices and fry till golden brown. Add 5½ cups of stock of the boiled mutton.
4. Add mutton pieces, red chilli powder, dhania powder, garam masala, and salt. Cook for 5 minutes.
5. When it starts boiling, add the rice and cook covered on low heat till each grain is separate and the water is absorbed.
6. Sprinkle orange colour on one half of the rice and yellow on the top of the other half. On top of the colours sprinkle kewra water and keep it on very low heat for about 5-10 minutes. Serve after about 15 minutes.

# Hyderabadi Murg Biryani

### Serves 6

2 cups uncooked long grain basmati rice
2 tej patta (bay leaves), 1½ tsp salt, 1 tbsp oil

**FOR THE CHICKEN**

1 chicken (700-800 gm) - cut into 12 pieces
4 large onions - chopped, 1½ tbsp ginger-garlic paste
2 large tomatoes - chopped
1 cup thick curd
1 tsp chilli powder, salt to taste, 5-6 tbsp oil

**GARNISHING**

1 cup sliced onions - fried till crisp and brown (2-3 large onions)
½ cup poodina leaves (whole)
few drops of orange colour or few strands kesar dissolved in 1 tsp warm water or
milk and 2-3 drops of kewra essence

*Shahi Tukri : Recipe on page 100* ➤

### FLAVOURING MASALA
1½ tsp jeera (cumin seeds), 3-4 chhoti illaichi (green cardamoms)
3-4 laung (cloves), 2" dalchini (cinnamon)
2-3 saboot kali mirch (peppercorns), 2 moti illaichi (black cardamoms)

### TEMPERING (TADKA)
3 tbsp ghee, ½ tsp shah jeera

1. To cook the rice, boil 6-7 cups of water with tej patta, salt, and oil. Add the rice and cook till almost tender. Strain and spread the drained rice on a wide tray. Run a fork through the rice to let the steam escape.
2. Heat oil in a heavy bottomed pan. Add chopped onions. Stir fry till golden brown. Add 1½ tbsp ginger-garlic paste. Stir for ½ minute.
3. Add chicken and bhuno on moderate flame for 3-4 minutes stirring continously. Add chopped tomatoes. Cook till dry.
4. Add curd. Stir for 2 minutes. Add salt and chilli powder. Mix well. Add 1 cup water and cook till chicken turns tender. If there is any extra curry, dry it on fire. Keep on fire till you get a thick masala gravy. Remove from fire. Keep aside.
5. Grind all the ingredients under flavouring masala by adding ¼ cup

water to get a paste. Add ½ cup water to the above paste and strain it. Keep liquid flavouring masala aside.

6. For assembling the biryani, take a large heavy bottomed pan, grease it. Sprinkle 3-4 tbsp masala gravy of the chicken at the bottom.

7. Spread 1/3 of the rice. Place ½ the chicken pieces on it and make the rice moist with 2-3 tbsp gravy.

8. Sprinkle 1/3 of the fried onion and pudina on it. Sprinkle 2-3 tbsp liquid flavouring masala.

9. Repeat by adding rice, then chicken, then masala gravy, followed by pudina and fried onions and flavouring masala. Finish with a top layer of rice sprinkled with some fried onions, pudina and flavouring masala and 2-3 drops of kewra and colour.

10. Heat ghee in a pan. Splutter jeera and pour on the biryani.

11. Cover the pan with a tight fitting lid and seal the lid with dough. Place the pan on fire with a tawa underneath to reduce the heat to minimum for ½ hour before serving.

**Note:** If a rich biryani is desired mix ½ cup cream with ½ cup yogurt and sprinkle 2-3 tbsp of this on each rice layer to keep rice moist.

# Subz Masala Pulao

*Picture on page* 103                    Serves 5-6

## PASTE

6-7 flakes garlic
1" piece ginger
1 tbsp saunf (aniseeds), 1 tsp jeera (cumin seeds)
3 dry, red chillies
1 tsp dhania (coriander) powder
1" stick dalchini (cinnamon), 3-4 laung (cloves)
3-4 saboot kali mirch (pepper corns)
seeds of 2 moti illaichi (brown cardamom)

## OTHER INGREDIENTS

2 cups basmati rice - soaked for 1 hour
1-2 carrots - peeled and cut diagonally into slices
1 small cauliflower - cut into medium florets
8-10 french beans - threaded and cut into 1" long diagonal pieces
2 small potatoes - cut into fours

1 tej patta (bay leaf), 2 onions - sliced finely
½ cup oil
3 tsp salt, 1 tsp lemon juice

1. Wash rice. Stain and let be in the strainer for atleast 30 minutes.
2. Grind the ingredients of the paste together with a little water.
3. Heat ½ cup oil in a heavy bottomed pan. Add tej patta and onions, cook till onions turn golden brown.
4. Add the vegetables and stir fry for 3-4 minutes.
5. Add the paste and stir to mix well.
6. Add 4 cups of water to the vegetables.
7. Add salt and lemon juice.
8. When water boils, add rice to the water.
9. Put a tawa under the pan of rice to reduce the heat further.
10. Cover the pan of rice with a small towel napkin and then with a well fitting lid. Keep some heavy weight on the lid.
11. Slow down the fire and cook till the rice is done (10-15 minutes).
12. Serve after 10 minutes.

# *Khumb Biryani*

### *Serves 4*

200 gms (1 packet) fresh mushrooms - cut into 4 pieces
2 medium sized boiled potatoes - cut into small cubes
2 onions - grind to a paste
10-15 flakes garlic and 2" piece ginger - ground to a paste (1½ tbsp)
¼ tsp haldi, ¾ tsp red chilli powder
1 tomato - chopped
3-4 tbsp chopped coriander
½ cup curd - beat till smooth
2 laung (cloves) - crushed

**RICE**
1 cup basmati rice - soaked for 20 minutes
1½ tsp salt
2 pinches of javitri (mace), 2-3 chhoti illaichi (green cardamom)
½" stick dalchini (cinnamon)

1. Boil 5-6 cups water with salt, javitri, chhoti illaichi and dalchini. Add the drained rice and cook till nearly done. (7-8 minutes). Keep checking while boiling the rice, if it is done. Do not over-cook rice. Drain rice and leave it uncovered. Separate the grains gently with a fork.
2. Heat 1 karchhi (4-5 tbsp) oil in a kadhai. Add onion paste and bhuno till oil separates and it turns golden brown.
3. Add ginger and garlic paste.
4. Add red chilli powder and haldi powder. Mix well
5. Add tomato and bhuno well till mashed and oil separates out.
6. Reduce flame. Add curd, stirring continuously to prevent curdling. Bhuno till the masala turns a little thick and oil separates.
7. Add crushed laung. Mix well
8. Add the chopped mushrooms to the masala and bhuno for 5 minutes on medium flame. Add salt and garam masala to taste. Mix in coriander.
9. Mix in the boiled, cubed potatoes. Bhuno for 1-2 minutes. Remove from fire.

*contd...*

10. To assemble the biryani, take a greased borosil dish. Spread half the mushroom-potato masala.
11. Spread half the rice on top of the khumb masala.
12. Spread the remaining vegetables and end finally with the leftover rice.
13. Heat 1 tbsp desi ghee and spread over the rice.
14. Sprinkle 2 pinches of javitri powder. Cover and seal with aluminium foil and keep on dum for 15-20 minutes in a slow oven at 100° C. Serve hot.

# *Missi Roti*

*Makes 6*  *Picture on page 75*

1 cup besan (gram flour)
1 cup atta (whole wheat flour)
2 tbsp oil or melted ghee
1 tbsp kasoori methi (dry fenugreek leaves)
½ tsp salt, ½ tsp red chilli powder
½ tsp jeera (cumin seeds)
a pinch of hing (asafoetida)
a pinch of haldi (turmeric powder)

1. Mix all ingredients. Add enough water to make a dough of rolling consistency. Cover it and keep aside for ½ hour.
2. Make 6 balls. Roll each ball into a chappati, but slightly thick.
3. Cook on a hot tawa by frying it or cook in a hot tandoor.
4. When made in a tandoor, apply ghee and serve immediately.

# *Lachha Parantha*

### *Makes 6*

3 cups atta (whole wheat flour)
3-4 tbsp ghee
½ tsp salt
2 tbsp chopped coriander

**PASTE**
2 tbsp ghee mixed with 1 tbsp maida

1. Mix atta with ghee and salt. Add coriander. Sprinkle water and knead well to a non sticky dough. Cover and keep aside for 1 hour.
2. Knead again and make 7-8 balls, the size of a lemon. Roll out each to a diameter of 8", almost as big as the chakla.
3. Spread some ghee-maida paste on it.
4. Pleat the chappati lengthwise into one collected strip.
5. Twist this strip.
6. Coil the strip to get a pedha (round flattened ball).

7. Flatten this ball between the palms of the hands or gently roll on the chakla (rolling board) with the belan (rolling pin) without applying too much pressure, to a small parantha of about 6" diameter.
8. Cook in a tandoor by applying water on the back side of the parantha. If you like you can cook it on a hot tawa also. To cook on a tawa first make both the sides light brown on a hot tawa. Reduce flame and then using ghee fry till rich brown on both sides on low heat. Press the sides and all over the parantha with a spoon while frying to ensure that it gets cooked since the parantha is a little thick.
9. Remove from tawa on to a clean kitchen napkin and press the hot parantha on the cloth from all sides for the layers to open up and turn flaky. Serve hot.

# *Tandoori Keema Parantha*

### *Serves 8*

250 gm keema (minced meat)
1 onion - chopped finely
2 tsp finely chopped ginger
1 tsp salt, 1 tsp dhania powder, ½ tsp red chilli powder, ½ tsp garam masala
2 green chillies - chopped, 1 tbsp finely chopped fresh coriander
1 tbsp kasoori methi (dry fenugreek leaves)

**DOUGH**
2 cups atta (wheat flour)
½ tsp salt, 1 tbsp ghee

1. To prepare the dough, sift flour and salt. Rub 1 tbsp ghee. Add enough water to make a dough. Cover and keep aside for 30 minutes.
2. To prepare the filling, heat 2 tbsp oil and fry the chopped onions until rich brown.

3. Add mince and ginger and mix well. Reduce heat. Add salt, dhania powder, red chilli powder and garam masala. Fry for 1-2 minutes. Cook covered on low heat for about 5 minutes, till the mince is cooked.
4. Add green chillies and 1 tbsp finely chopped coriander. If there is any water, uncover and dry the mince on fire. Keep the stuffing aside.
5. Divide the dough into 6 equal parts. Shape into round balls.
6. Flatten each ball, roll out each into a round of 5" diameter.
7. Spread 1 tsp full of ghee. Then spread 1-2 tbsp of filling all over.
8. Make a slit, starting from the centre till any one end.
9. Start rolling from the slit, to form an even cone.
10. Keeping the cone upright, press slightly.
11. Roll out, applying pressure only at the centre. Do not roll or press too much on the sides, otherwise the layers of parantha do not separate after cooking.
12. Sprinkle some kasoori methi and press with a rolling pin (belan).
13. Apply water on the back side of the parantha and stick carefully in a heated tandoor or place in a preheated oven in a greased tray.
14. Remove after a few minutes. Spread some ghee, serve hot.

# Meetha

# *Baadami Sewian Kheer*

### *Serves 5-6*

1 kg full cream milk
4 tbsp almonds-blanched (soaked & peeled), ground to a paste with some milk
1/3 cup sewian, ¼ cup sugar, or to taste, 1-2 drops kewra essence
1 tbsp each of shredded almonds and pistachios, 1-2 silver leaves

1. Blanch the almonds by soaking them in hot water, remove skins and grind almonds to a fine paste with a little milk.
2. Boil the leftover milk for 15 minutes on low heat. Add almond paste. Boil for 2-3 minutes.
3. Add the sewian and cook covered on slow fire for 5 minutes till they become tender and you get a kheer like consistency.
4. Add sugar, cook and stir continuously till the sugar dissolves well.
5. Remove from fire. Cool.
6. Add kewra essence. Decorate with silver leaves, shredded almonds and pistachios. Serve hot or cold.

# Shahi Tukri

*Golden crisp bread topped with rabri.*

*Picture on page 85*                         *Serves 6*

4 slices bread
2½ cups cold milk
¼ cup plus 1 tbsp sugar
5-6 chhoti illaichi (green cardamoms) - skinned and crushed
a few strands of kesar (saffron) dissolved in 1 tbsp water
75 gms khoya (dried whole milk)
4-5 almonds - cut into thin long pieces
4-5 pista (pistachio) - blanched and cut into thin long pieces
1 sliver leaf
4 tbsp desi ghee

1. Remove the side crusts of bread. Cut each slice into 3 pieces.
2. Fry bread in 4-5 tbsp ghee till golden brown. Dip in cold milk for a second. Remove fried slices from milk and arrange in a flat serving plate.
3. Heat the left over milk after soaking the bread, with sugar and chhoti illaichi. Boil. Reduce heat.
4. Mash khoya and add to the milk.
5. Cook this milk till it thickens and turns into a rabri (for about 15-20 minutes). Remove from fire and let it come to room temperature.
6. Pour the rabri over the toasts.
7. Decorate with silver leaf.
8. Sprinkle shredded almonds and pista. Dot with some soaked kesar.
9. Serve warm or cold, according to the weather.

# *Kesar Kulfi*

### *Serves 8*

1 kg (5 cups) full cream milk
½ cup sugar
2 tbsp cornflour
¼ tsp kesar - dissolved in 1 tbsp warm milk
75 gms fresh khoya - grated and mashed slightly
1 tbsp pista (pistachio) - very finely cut, 1 tbsp almonds - very finely cut
seeds of 3-4 chhoti illaichi (green cardamom) - crushed

1. Dissolve cornflour in 1 cup milk and keep aside.
2. Mix the rest of the milk with kesar in a kadhai. Boil till it is reduced to half in quantity, for about 20 minutes on medium fire.
3. Add illaichi, sugar and cornflour paste. Cook for 3-4 minutes more till the sugar is well dissolved. Remove from fire. Cool slightly.
4. Add khoya, almonds and pistas.
5. Fill the mixture in the kulfi moulds. Freeze for 6-8 hours or overnight.

***Subz Masala Pulao : Recipe on page 88*** ➤

# *Nita Mehta's* **BEST SELLERS**

**Favourite Non-Vegetarian** **Food for CHILDREN** **CONTINENTAL Non Veg.** **THAI Cookery**

 **MORE DESSERTS**

**Taste of RAJASTHAN** **MORE DESSERTS** **Low Calorie Recipes** **Microwave Non-Veg**

 **The Best of CHICKEN Recipes**

**SNACKS Non Veg.** **The Best of CHICKEN Recipes** **Taste of KASHMIR** **BREAKFAST Non Veg.**